A GOD
TO DESIRE

A God to Desire

A Handbook for Spiritual Growth
by Blake Steele

Copyright © 2003 Scandinavia Publishing House
Drejervej 11-21, DK 2400 Copenhagen NV, Denmark
Tel.: (45) 35310330   Fax: (45) 35310334   E-Mail: jvo@scanpublishing.dk
Text copyright © 2003 Blake Steele
Photo copyright © 2003 Blake Steele
Design by Ben Alex
Hubble space photos © STScl/NASA

Printed in Singapore
ISBN 87 7247 261 8

SPIRITUAL VISION SERIES

by Blake Steele

A God to Desire
Being Loved
Radical Forgiveness
Creative Compassion

A GOD TO DESIRE

A HANDBOOK FOR SPIRITUAL GROWTH

WORDS AND PHOTOGRAPHY
BY BLAKE STEELE

scandinavia

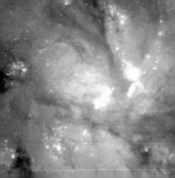

This book series is designed to enhance spiritual healing and transformation. Through a unique blend of words and images, scripture, poems and exercises, it gives you tools to take spiritual reality from a mental understanding to a heart experience where all the good things happen.

A God To Desire points to a beautiful God of infinite Love. The God who created this vast universe is always in every way greater than we can imagine. This is the God who is intimately here, the fountain of Life that makes us fully alive.

As we grow more spiritually receptive to a God more loving than we can imagine we awake to the wonder of an open, spiritual universe, full of beauty, alive with God. This is the kingdom of heaven that Jesus proclaimed.

I hope this little book becomes a warm companion and helpful tool for you on your journey towards spiritual freedom.

BLAKE STEELE

We only need to open our eyes and look around to realize the Creator of this amazing universe is always, in all His attributes and ways, far beyond our understanding.

The inconceivable energies of stars and galaxies reflect a mere fraction of the power of God's being, for God is infinite in power.

How great is God — beyond our understanding! Job 36:26

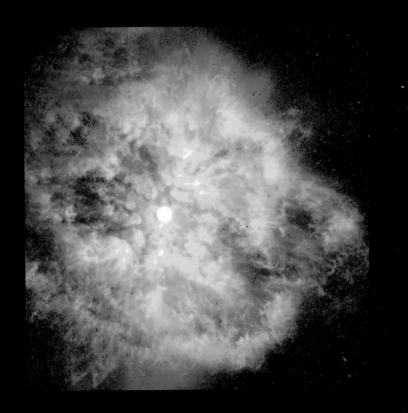

God is beautiful, more beautiful than we can imagine, for all the beauty of Creation streams forth from His infinite, beautiful mind.

HE BRINGS OUT THE STARS, ONE BY
ONE AND CALLS EACH OF THEM BY
NAME. ISAIAH 40:26

To whom can we compare the Maker who spoke the billion gleaming galaxies, Creator of Earth and everything in it, eternal and fathomless in all His attributes?

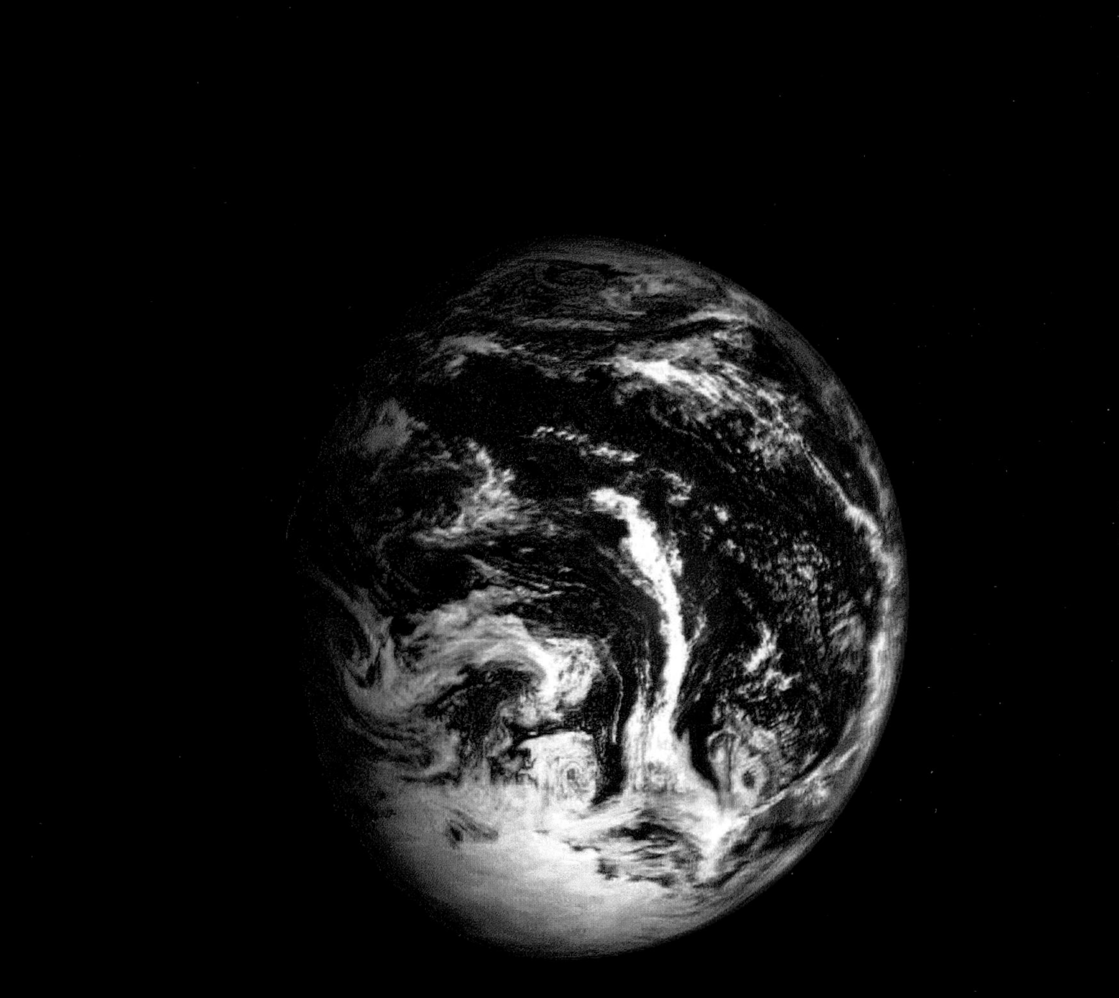

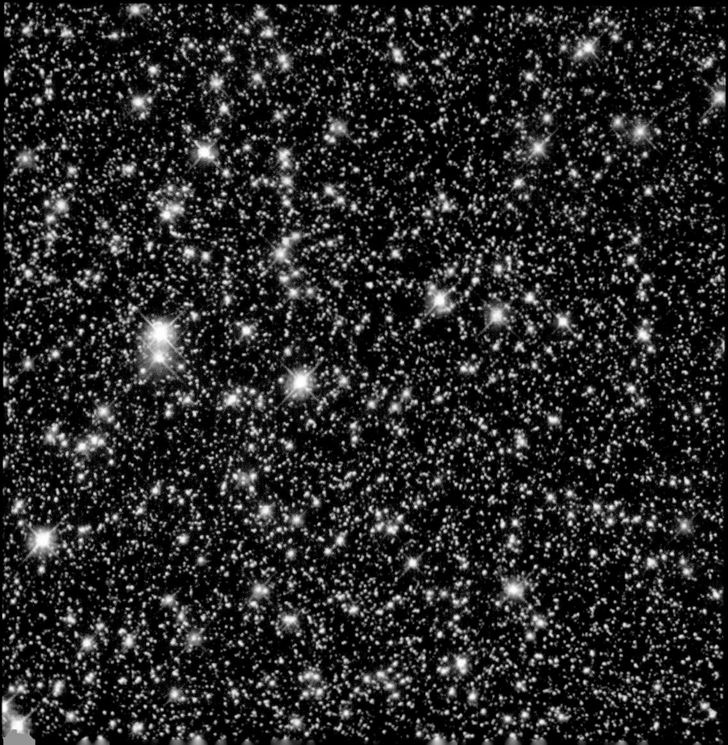

God lives beyond the dimensions of time and space. To think of God in terms of time is to limit His eternity; to think in spatial terms is to limit His infinite being. God creates but is uncreated, the source of existence, a being of limitless wisdom and Love in whom the whole expansive universe exists and who is everywhere present.

GOD... WHO IS OVER ALL
AND THROUGH ALL AND IN
ALL. EPH 4:6

15

The poets of Scripture portray a God both transcendently great and intimately here, busily involved in His world.

He makes the grass grow, the snow blow, the sun shine, the wind wend; God rides on the clouds of the sky and walks on the wings of the wind. He sends streams out of the mountains and waters the earth from His chambers. He opens His hands and feeds the fish of the sea and animals of forests and fields. He is here, making everything be and happen.

This is the spiritual language of poetry expressing an ineffable paradox of truth: that the free working of a wondrous universe exists within a transcendent God who expresses Himself to us through creation. This is a God who is robust with Life and delights in all He has made.

DID NOT HE WHO MADE ME IN THE WOMB MAKE THEM? DID NOT THE SAME ONE FORM US BOTH WITHIN OUR MOTHERS? JOB 31:15

Each of us slipped into this world out of the hands of God: born innocent and eager for life's colors to splash our blank infant minds. God was there, loving us, in the miraculous instant of life, longing for Love to spill out upon us, to bless us and bless us, slather us in blessing, so we could grow: exploring, open and wondering, laughing at being human, laughing at being so close to God.

HE IS NOT FAR FROM ANY OF US, FOR IN HIM WE LIVE AND MOVE, AND HAVE OUR BEING. ACTS 17:28

God is here, closer than breathing, more intimate than your heart beat, more real than the thoughts and feelings that deny Him. He is the fountain of existence.

FOR HIS SPIRIT HAS MADE US; HIS BREATH HAS GIVEN US LIFE. JOB 33:4

21

Once a little fish asked a lobster, "Do you believe there is an ocean?"

"Of course I believe there is an ocean," answered the lobster.

"I believe there is an ocean too," the fish replied. "I only wish I could find it. I've heard it is wonderful and mysterious beyond belief. If I could find the ocean I know I would be happy."

"But, this is the ocean. We are in it right now."

"Oh no. That can't be, the little fish said. "Everybody knows this is only water."

Our brains sleep deep in the miracle of God.

YOU SEND FORTH YOUR SPIRIT,
AND THEY ARE CREATED. Ps 104:30

Scripture reveals that every human being, every bird that cracks an egg, every baby gazelle miraculously birthed and laid glistening on the ground comes into being from God. Here the miracle of life is recognized as issuing straight out of God.

Life, life—what is life after all? Even the most advanced sciences cannot fathom the bright mystery of consciousness. We are full of a miracle we cannot comprehend.

26

27

IN HIM WAS LIFE; AND THE LIFE WAS THE LIGHT OF MEN. THE LIGHT SHINES IN THE DARKNESS, AND THE DARKNESS CANNOT COMPREHEND IT. JOHN 1:4,5

Jesus came. The man stood like a flame of God, luminous of spirit, loving in being... showing the essence, the nature of life.

28

AND THE LIFE WAS MANIFESTED... AND THIS IS THE MESSAGE WE HEARD FROM HIM, THAT GOD IS LIGHT... I JOHN 1:2, 5

In Christ life older than stars and eternally young flowed as free as the wind through a man—God's boundless being of Light was clothed in clay.

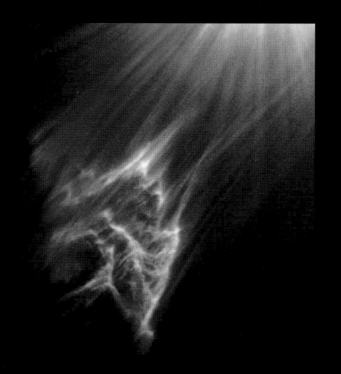

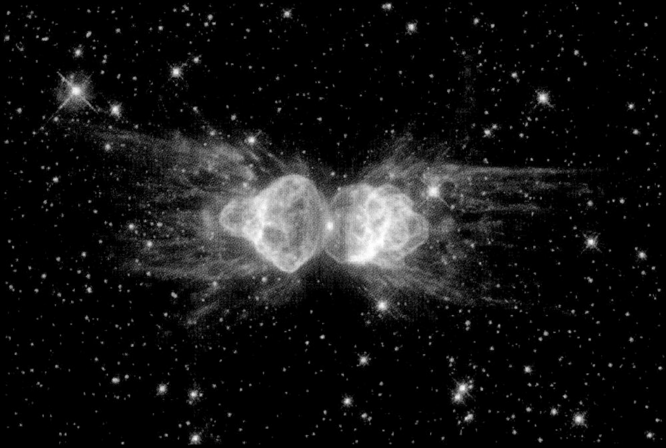

The Son of Man came and gave voice to the eternal wisdom and power who created all things, sustains all things, holds all things together. And He is the essence of this wisdom—the Son of God.

FOR IN HIM ALL THINGS WERE
CREATED, IN THE HEAVENS
AND ON EARTH, VISIBLE AND
INVISIBLE... ALL THINGS HAVE
BEEN CREATED THROUGH HIM
AND FOR HIM. ...AND IN HIM
ALL THINGS HOLD TOGETHER.
COL 1:16-17

Every atom holds together by His power, every molecule in your body exists in His Light. All the wisdom working within every cell of your body is busily working in the patterns of His divine wisdom.

If it were possible to take a picture of the Milky Way from deep space and make a photographic print as big as North America, our solar system, from the sun to Pluto, would measure only 2 inches across. And the Milky Way is but one of 100 billion galaxies. Yet Christ is greater than Creation—for the entire universe, in all its dimensions, from galaxies to quarks, from amebas to archangels, exists within His infinite fields of wisdom and power.

...CHRIST, THROUGH WHOM ARE ALL THINGS... I COR 8:6

God is transcendent and limitless. Christ is greater than we can conceive. And God in Christ is here—life flowing out of Him; closer than we have imagined, brimming with brightness, alive, aware, creative and caring—the uncreated Light we cannot see, filling all we thought was empty space.

God is the transparency we are looking through.

34

We live in the naked radiance of God, in the total openness of divine light, in a universal fountain, in the slow gush called life rushing from heaven back to heaven at the speed of Love. And we are unaware... We are like bats flying blind into a lake of light.

The infinite Creator who is intimately here is the God the prophets wrote of and Jesus revealed, but centuries of interpretations and religious traditions have clouded with countless connotations and limitations. We have progressively domesticated and diminished the God who is alive and free. Instead of waking up to Him in all our ways we have squeezed the Maker out of His creation in our theology and thinking.

Though God reveals Himself through the limits of language in order to be understood, He never intended that we should limit Him.

It is human nature to diminish God—to make Him less than He is— while it is God's nature to expand humanity—to make us more than we are. God became man that we might become fully alive in God.

38

In the gospels we see Jesus blowing open the possibilities and demonstrating what life can be in union with God. Jesus wants us to have a big, beautiful God in a big, beautiful universe.

Christ came to illuminate humanity's understanding as He revealed God to be creative, compassionate Love that can transform our deep hearts and free us.

The power of God poured through Jesus to those who recognized their need for His Love. These were the openhearted ones to whom the possibilities of God were revealed.

39

Jesus spoke: the blind saw, the mute spoke, shriveled bodies unwrinkled in the light; a crippled woman danced; a young boy with a tormented mind laughed again. Jesus rose a little girl from the dead; calmed a storm; walked on top of the sea; fed 5,000 with five loaves of bread; changed water into wine. Through Christ, Love's pure, creative potential transformed energy, freed life.

And when they killed Him—He was so spangled full of life—He burst back through the tomb into infinite realms of God's beauty. Jesus showed us in every act and word that this is a spiritual universe, open to God's beauty and wonder, where everything He did is possible, and more.

I AM THE LIGHT OF THE WORLD;
HE WHO FOLLOWS ME SHALL HAVE
THE LIGHT OF LIFE. JOHN 8:12

God is always more wonderful than we think in every aspect and way. Spiritual growth is therefore a process of unlimiting God and our selves. It is a life-long process of confronting and outgrowing our inner resistance to the abundant potential and free nature of God.

And it is waking up from mental spells that cause us to define our lives according to need rather than the miracle of existance and the Love that is our destiny.

AWAKE, AWAKE, AND PUT ON YOUR
BEAUTIFUL GARMENTS... Is 52:1

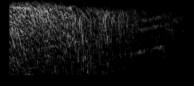

45

WAKE UP, O SLEEPER... AND CHRIST
WILL SHINE ON YOU. EPH 5:14

The face of God is hidden in everything—Only Love reveals Him.

Once there was a monk named Brother Lawrence. One day, while looking at a tree, he suddenly saw the actual wonder of it, unfiltered by his mental concepts—and he woke up to God. From that day on he lived aware of God's presence amidst his daily chores. Wonder opened him to God and God poured Love through his heart. He wrote his experiences in a spiritual classic, *The Practice of the Presence of God.*

God is here, but we are asleep in a world of mental judgments and misconceptions. Sense the miracle of anything, a tree, a bird, the sky, your body—be a child again—your heart will open and you will know that the kingdom of God is at hand.

Blue sky... Be Amazed!
Budding branch... Celebrate!
Bird on the branch...
Blow me away with Praises!

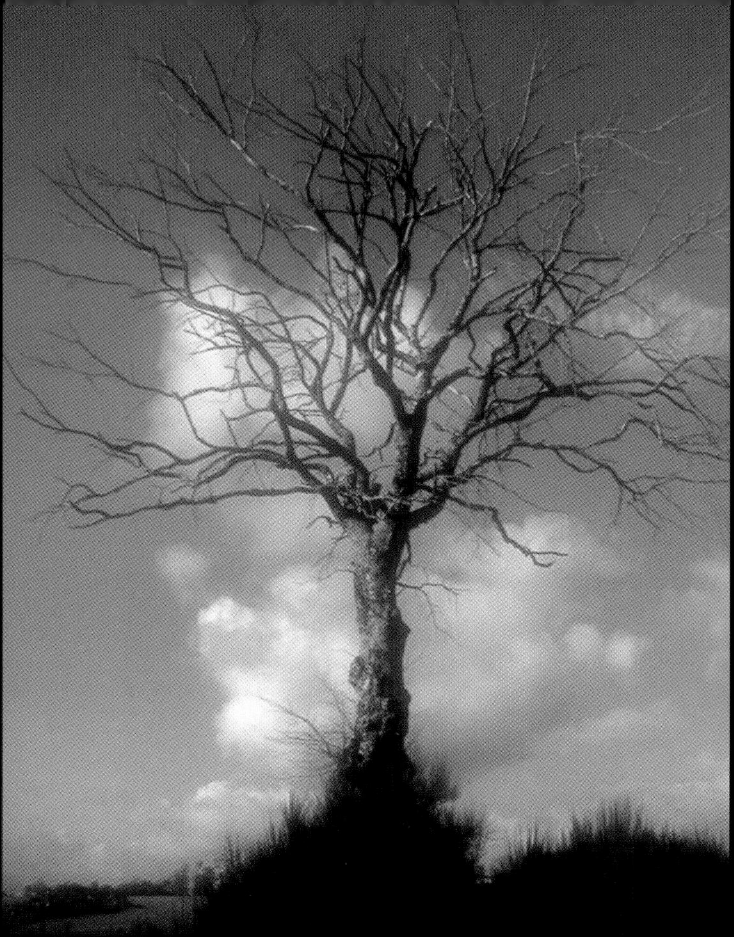

The infinite God is intimately with us, waiting to pour through our opening hearts, loving us far more than we have the capacity to receive.

It is God I love pouring through opening things.
God the glory pouring down, gushing up, flooding out.
When all people let God through,
it shall be a revolution of truth's beauty.

Grace is the way of unconditional Love.

> THE LAW WAS GIVEN THROUGH MOSES,
> BUT GRACE AND TRUTH CAME THROUGH
> JESUS CHRIST. JOHN 1:14,16

Grace was Jesus' revolution, bringing a powerful turning point in mankind's understanding of himself and God.

Under old religious systems based on human efforts to be good, we remain consciously separate from God. God is "out there" somewhere, judging us, and we are "down here" trying to keep all the rules. Yet it is precisely our sense of disconnectedness that is the source of our deepest insecurity, and the greatest attainment of self's effort to be righteous can only be self-righteousness—the thing Jesus stood most strongly against.

53

BY GRACE YOU ARE SAVED, THROUGH
FAITH... IT IS THE GIFT OF GOD... EPH 2:8

But grace is God's unearnable gift of forgiveness and freedom: it is
the doors thrown open, the weary prodigal warmly welcomed
home, our hearts united to His river of blessing. Grace is the free
gift of the union that heals us. The soul returns home to its true
center in God.

*We are released by His radical forgiveness of grace into the
outpouring Spirit of grace, into a life of healing in grace, unto the
fullness of freedom in grace.*

Through simple acceptance we grow by the complete free gift of it.

The heart's freedom
is its open surrender
to the breath of God.

The self that wants to play God or be righteous resists by nature the free gift-giving nature of grace. It just doesn't make sense to the mind nurtured by its sense of separation. But grace is about union, becoming receptive to the excessive, lush folly of Love: it evokes liberation. Grace makes the soul beautiful with God.

A crazy man thought he had to earn sunshine.
He worked hard, but after a while
it didn't make sense, even to him.
Then he thought that if he hid in the shadows
the sun would cease to exist. That didn't work.
So then he determined to spit out the sun.
That didn't work either.
Finally, he laid down and got a tan.

59

Once we grasp the free nature of grace, and that openhearted receptivity is our only possible relationship to it, we realize it is our job to stop trying to be good, and to yield to a relationship of divine Love loving us. Being loved and drinking grace into our heart makes us warm and savory with His goodness and brings peace to our souls.

Many sincere religious people don't understand the implications of grace and are still trying hard to be good for God. Ironically, they are resisting God's grace in religious ways.

Our work in grace is to overcome our anxious resistance to grace.

God is the infinite wellspring of blessing, pouring out gifts, giving and brimming, bestowing and blessing, and loving to bless in the rivers of blessing.

IF YOU PRACTICE MY TEACHINGS... THEN
YOU WILL KNOW THE TRUTH, AND THE
TRUTH WILL MAKE YOU FREE. JOHN 8:31,32

It is practicing the transformational truth of Christ that frees us to
be robust with life and makes the Light of life arise in our eyes.

All things have been created by Love to be transformed by Love
into the beauty of Love. This is the great truth we must wake up
to: that we are by nature creative and transformative and designed
for Love, and God is waiting for us to freely give ourselves to
Love's instincts and ways.

IT IS FOR FREEDOM THAT
CHRIST SETS US FREE. GALATIANS 5:1

63

64

65

Christ can free us from resistance to the Loving, pure freedom of God, from whose boundless being flows unconditional Love in rivers of delight.

YOU GIVE THEM DRINK FROM THE RIVER OF YOUR PLEASURE. FOR WITH YOU IS THE FOUNTAIN OF LIFE; IN YOUR LIGHT WE SEE LIGHT. Ps 36:8,9

And He is able to transform our minds to think in the creative patterns of His Love, for how else can we be truly renewed?

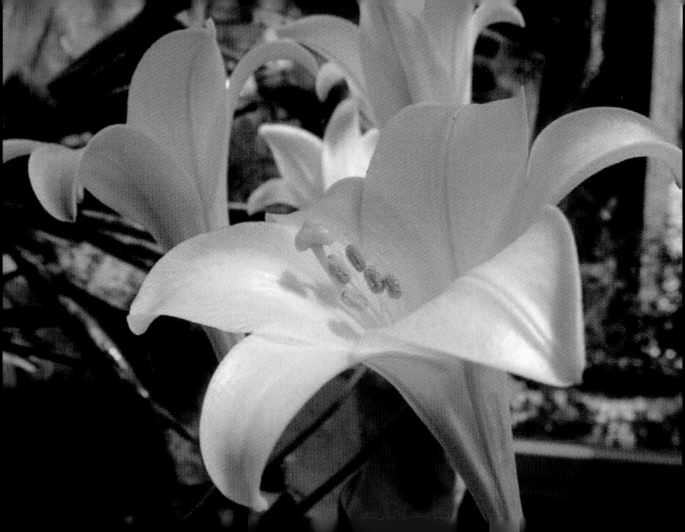

Ultimately, Truth is not a mental construct in our minds, it is not rigid, or abstract, nor dead—or something our ego can ever own—for Truth is the reality that creates our minds and bodies, birds and stones, nebulas birthing new stars and the light in your eyes.

And Truth is the way of life that must be lived to be fully known—for it is the soul that undoes its resistance to Love that drinks deeply from the river of Life and is renewed.

Truth in Christ is not a burdensome thing, but a delicious, expansive awakening for the soul with a passion to wake up in the freshness of God and be free.

Young Joy laughing,
the Lamb laughing in me:
God laughing at the miracle
of a heart opening.
The Holy Spirit gurgles up.
I am laughing in a clean river,
laughing like a child
in the freedom of Love.

GOD IS SPIRIT... JOHN 4:24
The spiritual journey is opening the heart unto God who is Spirit; becoming alive in He who is an infinite sea of radiant Life—the great Love who births all things.

CHRIST IS A LIFE-GIVING SPIRIT... I COR 15:45
And it is knowing Christ as a life-giving Spirit who seeks us, forgives us fully, and heals us with Love when our hearts open to Him.

THE HOLY SPIRIT POURS GOD'S LOVE INTO OUR HEARTS... ROM 5:5
And it is receiving His Spirit that is older than stars, fresher than sea spray, silently spacious in a free-flowing nature, eternal and luminous in the moment of life—pouring Love.

WHERE THE SPIRIT OF THE LORD IS,
THERE IS FREEDOM. II COR. 3:17

God is utterly free. When a heart opens and lets His Spirit flow
through, a spontaneous outflow of life happens. It is His Spirit that
can dissolve the darkness out of us—if we will only let go.

The Holy Spirit is a fountain,
bubbling up, crystalline,
welling up, laughing—
flowing through us
from eternity to eternity.

Paul's life was revolutionized by the Spirit's freedom. He wrote that the New Covenant is not of letters written with ink on paper or stone... but is of the Spirit, written on human hearts... *for the letter kills, but the Spirit gives life.* (II Cor 3)

Where is God writing His New Covenant? On your heart, for this is the Covenant of Love transforming us. It is about a new heart: clean, open, spacious, and spiritual.

You are Love's letter for others to read.

78

We open our being to the luminous Spirit—
the radiant river flows.
Christ rises in us like fragrance from a field
of young roses.

As the Love of Christ dissolves our mental veils and washes our deep heart, our eyes begin to open: nothing is ordinary anymore—the common bush begins to burn—for when Love unites with beauty in our heart, the face of God, hidden in the secret glory of the world, begins to be revealed.

THEN YOU WILL SEE AND BE RADIANT; YOUR HEART WILL THROB AND SWELL WITH JOY. Is 60:5

There is a great mystery hidden in everything; and as our minds are transformed our awareness keeps opening. The God we thought was gone away, or stodgy, or dead, is here! alive—silent and peaceful, bursting and bubbling—and everything changes.

81

My own journey of transformation has been so amazing. I struggled for a long time before I realized that the only thing I can really do is surrender, let go, open my heart, let God be. At times it has been so painful to face myself honestly, to accept that I have so much self-delusion, and in a way even harder to forgive and accept myself completely—but spiritual reality is so worth it. To live in this world with an open heart to God is the "pearl of precious price". Life really is an astonishing miracle.

When your heart opens wide, centered in His Light, the world becomes more alive than you ever imagined it could be: colors burn, sounds sing, and every breath you take seems to expand and fill your whole body with vitality and spacious freedom; the Spirit rises and bubbles through your soul, and Love becomes the reality of your life. The world needs your happiness. You really can step out of old ways and become part of Christ's answer—this quiet revolution of Love.

84

The Great Love opens the body and mind.
The Great Love shines.
Old ugliness melts away
in young, secret sunlight.
The beauty of the world becomes
more beautiful and Spirit pours.

This is a universe alive with God's glory—the kingdom of heaven is here! waiting for us to wake up in Love, by Love, for Love–to be washed in His pure Spirit of Life that can flow through every cell of our bodies. Christ Jesus, who is eternally alive, is waiting for our simple choice, our commitment to live with open hearts, receiving the pure Love and beauty of God.

The child of grace believes
in the God of Love and plays.
The child of Love believes
in the sudden intrusion of beauty.
To have such a simple heart
must be like a heaven walking on earth.

The only person we can change in this world is our self.
By yielding to the ways of spiritual transformation, each of us can grow increasingly receptive to a God more loving than we can imagine and wake up amidst the wonders of an open, spiritual universe, full of beauty, alive with God.

For God is a wonder of spiritual beauty
and Love is the mystery and law of Creation.
All things exist to be transformed by Love.

91

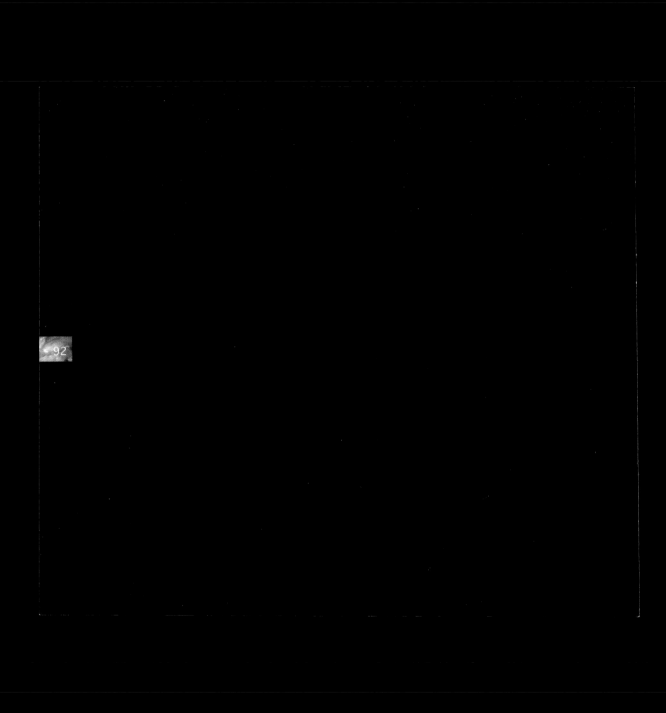

92

WORK BOOK

Because it is the free working of God's Spirit that makes us grow and not our own efforts, spiritual exercises become methods of unblocking ourselves and developing openhearted receptivity and responsiveness to the grace and freedom of God in Christ.

The effects of genuine spiritual practice are: a growing sense of God's presence, clarification of our minds, increasing freedom from inner conflicts and bondages, joy in the wonder of life, becoming utterly honest, inner rest and harmony, and living from our depths, with our whole selves, in Love.

This workbook section touches on several major spiritual practices recorded in the Bible. These are ancient and time-honored ways that are life changing when practiced with a clear intention to open our hearts to the wonder of He who loves us limitlessly. Each section gives a brief overview of a specific practice and a spiritual exercise.

PRAYER

Traditionally, prayer is simply communicating with God. It emphasizes otherness: us speaking to our Maker. It can range from simply talking about daily things to sharing with Him the deepest hopes and griefs of our lives. It can be formal and communal or spontaneous and deeply intimate, but always, true prayer is utterly sincere and from the heart.

The Hebrew words translated pray and prayer in the Bible imply making strong requests and interceding for another. The Greek word most used in the New Testament means to wish to God your hopes, yearnings, and aspirations.

WHATEVER YOU ASK FOR IN PRAYER, BELIEVE THAT YOU
HAVE RECEIVED IT, AND IT WILL BE YOURS. MARK 11:24

Jesus taught prayer as asking for very specific things with full confidence that God will honor our requests. This form of prayer is about manifesting what is possible. He taught that doubt and unforgiveness block manifestation, and trust in God and forgiveness from the heart release it. We all doubt, but thankfully the doubts and unforgiveness that block God's work can be progressively undone.

ASK, AND IT SHALL BE GIVEN TO YOU...
FOR EVERYONE WHO ASKS RECEIVES... MATT 7:7,8

The first step in this process is becoming very clear and specific with our requests. God wants to co-create with you. If you are vague, God will wait. Once you become specific the process will progress.

AND THIS IS THE CONFIDENCE THAT WE HAVE TOWARD HIM, THAT IF WE ASK ANYTHING ACCORDING TO HIS WILL, HE HEARS US... I JOHN 5:14

The second step is developing a pure intention. God is Love, and we are to ask according to His will. His will is for the nature of His Love to be expressed. Within God's nature there are limitless possibilities. Ask freely. Why not allow the increasing blessings of His Love?

AND WHENEVER YOU STAND PRAYING FORGIVE,
IF YOU HAVE ANYTHING AGAINST ANYONE... MARK 11:25

Forgive others, forgive yourself, forgive God, forgive the world—forgive completely and freely. Forgiveness is freedom and it is through a state of open-hearted freedom that prayer is most quickly manifested.

It is asking for very specific things with a clear, loving intention and the will to forgive that causes us to confront the doubts and self-judgments that block us. The following exercise will help you to break through these things to a full surrender of trust that allows God to work.

AND EVERYTHING YOU ASK IN PRAYER, BELIEVING, YOU SHALL RECEIVE. MATT 21:22

1. Write down everything you value and the reasons why. Take your time with this. Explore your heart and give form to it.
2. Write down your heart-felt wishes of good for yourself and others—especially those who have hurt you. Begin to break through negative attitudes with grace.

3. Make a list of what you would really like to accomplish before you die. If you don't know, start somewhere, anywhere. Dream big and small. Just start and more light will be given. Get it moving.

4. Now make a very specific prayer request list.

5. Ask God once, very clearly, to manifest the things on this list.

6. Accept that they are put in your spiritual bank account the minute you ask. You can do this by thanking God they are yours. Acceptance and thankfulness are the same thing.

7. Every day give thanks and affirm these requests as already yours. Keep the requests fully and clearly in your mind and heart.

8. During this process freely acknowledge the doubts that arise concerning your requests. Don't try to push them away. Doubt has its reasons and is often linked to past disappointments or false beliefs. Honestly question them concerning what is actually true. This is the way to undo them. Bring all within you openly to God. Be real. What is true makes us free. What is false binds us. Once you recognize a belief that binds and limits you it is just the opposite that is probably the truth, so write the belief down then turn it around by writing down the opposite. Look at both statements. How does each belief make you feel? Make a firm choice which statement you will embrace from now on.

Through this process God will help you resolve doubt until you come to peace in trust. (See Radical Forgiveness book of this series for more help.)

9. As doubts are undone your heart will rest more solidly assured that God hears your prayers. Your requests will become a solid part of your life, an inseparable part of your growth and destiny.

10. Surrender to God every expectation of when, where, with whom or how your prayers will be answered. This is the adventure of faith. It is through surrender that you make space for God to work.

11. Be flexible. Be free. Let God adjust your dreams. He is revealing and forming your deepest, truest self through this process.

12. Don't try to change those you are praying for, rather offer them complete acceptance. Make space for God to do His work in His own time and way. Continue to develop your openness to God through the other practices listed.

Meditation

In the Bible, the Hebrew words for *meditation* mean to murmur to yourself, ponder deeply and imagine; and in the Greek to revolve a matter around in your mind with care.

Biblical meditation often involves speaking a scripture aloud to yourself repeatedly, but also pondering something deeply and imaginatively, looking at it from different angles. This form of meditation takes words from the more rational levels of the mind into the deep mind, or heart. When our deep mind accepts something, things will shift in our lives in an almost miraculous way.

Scripture came through the divine inspiration of poets and prophets. The Old Testament was written in Hebrew. Jesus spoke Aramaic that was later translated into Greek. Both Hebrew and Aramaic are poetic languages of possibilities. One word can have many, often opposite meanings. Because of this it is an ancient Jewish spiritual practice to ponder the many possible meanings of the words of a prophet.

To experience Biblical meditation and something of the richness of the original languages I encourage you to get a good Bible concordance and dig into the possible meanings of a saying in the original languages. It is like mining for hidden gold. Pay attention to the roots of the words as well. You will be greatly rewarded with a whole new perspective. Here is an example from a saying of Jesus:

Come unto me you who work yourself to exhaustion and are sinking down under a heavy weight and I will stop you and reverse you and flood you with rest. For my union gives what is needed in a gracious way, and my work is to carry you along in lightness. Matt 11: 28-30

Exercise: Take this saying or any verse that calls to you and murmur it softly to yourself. Repeat various words and phrases to absorb their meaning. Open your heart and pray them to God. Ponder other possible meanings. Revolve the matter around in your mind letting it flash insights and inspirations into your heart.

Waiting on God

MY SOUL WAITS IN SILENCE FOR GOD ONLY. FROM HIM IS MY SALVATION.
Ps 62:1 (This word *salvation* in the Hebrew means *to be opened wide and made free.*)

The Hebrew words translated *waiting on God* mean *to gather your self, to interweave with God, to patiently watch, to know nothing and be astonished, to hope, to stop, to quiet yourself and wait in silence.*

Waiting on God is an ancient spiritual practice that has been to a great degree lost in the west. Whereas prayer involves our sense of distinction from God, waiting on God is about realizing our union.

IN THAT DAY YOU WILL KNOW... YOU ARE IN ME AND I IN YOU. JOHN 14:20

It is this rhythm of union and distinction that brings a wholeness and richness of being into full birth. It is God's work to free us in this dynamic blend of union and uniqueness. He is the vine; we are the branches. Eternal life is knowing we are One Life with Him.

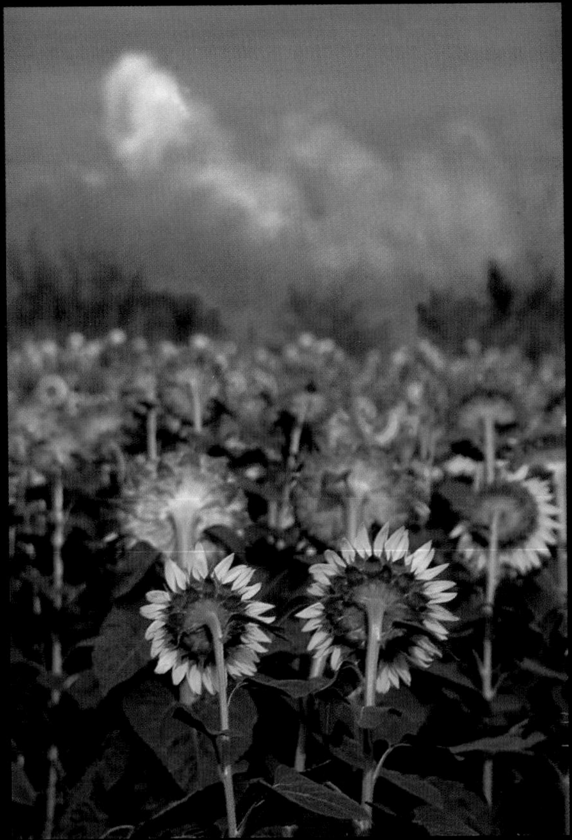

IN RETURNING TO REST SHALL YOU BE SAVED (OPENED WIDE AND MADE FREE). IN STILLNESS AND CONFIDENCE SHALL COME YOUR MASTERY. Is 30:15

Exercise: Sit quietly. Open your heart to God. You can do this through prayer or meditation on a scripture verse. After you sense His presence, simply put your hand over your heart and rest your attention there. Thank God for living in your deepest heart, beyond your body, beyond emotions, beyond your thoughts, beyond molecules, open, spacious, a silent ocean of infinite Love. Imagine an open door in your heart and His Light shining through.

Now notice how your thoughts arise and fall spontaneously in your mind. See them like little children playing, sometimes arguing, sometimes running off, sometimes sulking. As you breathe in let your breath carry your thoughts through the door of your heart into the spaciousness and silence of God's presence to dissolve away in rest. With your out-breath allow His silence to flow out and permeate your mind, blessing all your thoughts with grace and peace.

Now imagine God as your Father, standing at the door and welcoming his children home. With your in-breath you say, "Come home thought to your source.

Come home to God's rest." Whether the children have been fighting or playing, lazy or productive, it doesn't matter—they are all wandering children needing to come home to His Love. Kiss and welcome each one.

With the in-breath you bring them home to dissolve away in rest like so many streams brought back to the ocean from which they came. With the out-breath you are allowing vastness, silence, and the wonder of God's presence to burst forth as Lord into the field of thought, fresh, spontaneous, full of Love. Wait on God only in silence. Be opened wide and made free.

Eyes of the Heart
In the New Testament, Paul prays for believers that, *the eyes of your heart may be enlightened, that you might know the hope of your calling... and riches of His glory in us.* (Ephesians 1:18) In Greek this phrase, the *eyes of your heart being enlightened,* means to inwardly gaze at your mind's focused thought or imaginative imagery that is (opened to and) shining with God's light.

Our imagination is our God-given creative capacity. The language of our deep heart is not rational thought but imaginative imagery and emotion. Imaginative imagery and the emotions it evokes are just as real to our deep heart as impute from our physical senses. It is what we have imagined and felt about our experiences that have formed the beliefs and self-judgments that form us. So it is through the use of imaginative imagery and emotions that we can be transformed.

You don't need to spend much time with an Eyes of the Heart meditation. It is the quality of your time and regular repetition that have a transformative effect. The key is, don't try to change your emotions, just freely change the imaginative imagery you connect to them and the emotions will also change. This shift of focus from emotions to imaginative imagery gives you power and creative control over all that is within your deep heart. Exercise the eyes of your heart regularly and God's Spirit will undo deeply held negative beliefs and emotions and fill your heart with Love and beauty—the riches of His glory.

Here are three simple meditations to help you get started. You can use any imagery that makes sense to you or images from a scripture that calls to you in a visual way. Keep it simple. Let it come alive.

AND HE WILL SIT AS A PURIFIER OF SILVER... AND REFINE THEM
LIKE GOLD AND SILVER... MAL 3:3

Exercise: When you feel a negative emotion connected to an inner negative belief imagine your heart as a pool of molten gold. See the emotion as a dark spot floating upon the surface. Scoop off the dark spot and throw it into a bucket of fire. Now see the gold of your heart shining bright and clear as the sun. (Song of Songs 6:10) Give thanks and praise.

Exercise: Whenever you feel a negative emotion imagine it as a dark cloud being sucked out of you by a powerful vacuum cleaner and deposited in a golden bowl with the word *Truth* written on it. Watch the dark cloud dissolve away in the bowl of truth until nothing remains but a shining, golden bowl.

AND HE SHOWED ME A RIVER OF THE WATER OF LIFE, CLEAR AS CRYSTAL... REV 22:1

Exercise: Imagine a bright river flowing by. See yourself standing by a crystal clear pool in the river. You have a heavy backpack on and your arms are full of packages, Dive in and feel the fresh bubbling water with your whole body. Now imagine the wet, heavy packages and the backpack pulling you down.

Let go of the packages, one by one. As you do, feel yourself getting lighter and freer. Imagine your heaviest burden in the backpack. Take it off. Spread your arms out wide in complete surrender and let the river effortlessly carry you along.

The Spiritual Exercise of Wonder
Developing our sense of awe regarding this incredible Universe is a powerful spiritual practice. Awe is the beginning of wisdom. Wonder is a doorway to the sacred. When we glimpse His face in Love and awe, we are enlightened.

Exercise: Slow down. Take time to sense the artistry of God moving through all things: plants, stones, water and fire, clouds and open sky. Sense growing things and the goodness of God's earth. Ponder the patient trees. Look up and feel the warmth of the sun or the cool gray of clouds. Gaze into an animal's innocent eyes. Watch birds fly. Watch a child's free movements. Sense the unique soul Christ loves looking at you through another person's eyes. Remember that the whole Universe is a gift of His Love given for you to grow in wisdom and wonder and in your capacity to be loved and to love.

Whenever you sense the wonder, whisper to the Lord, *I cannot praise You as You deserve to be praised.* Stay with this until you feel something melt inside.

Combine Spiritual Exercises
Exercise: Read this book again, slowly, with the intent to go deeper into what it has to say through a combination of these spiritual practices. Prayerfully meditate in it. Let imaginative imagery develop in your heart from the various scriptures, poems and text. Stop and wait silently on God when you sense His presence. Go out into Creation. Touch His glory. Be fully alive.

Blake Steele is one of God's vagabonds on earth, traveling to do creative work and share God's abundant love through personal encounters and workshops. A versatile artist, he has written over 2,000 poems, a novel, children's stories, is a lyricist for choral pieces and a photographer. In this book series, he shares his vision, wisdom and awe for God through photography and poetic writing.

www.beingloved.net